# TRUE COVID 19 IN 2020 WHO IS CORONA? WHAT IS CORONA?

THE FAMOUS PROFESSIONAL GREAT WRITER
and a GREAT AUTHOR

## MR. JAMES EARL HARRIS

AuthorHouse™
1663 Liberty Drive
Bloomington, IN 47403
www.authorhouse.com
Phone: 833-262-8899

This book is printed on acid-free paper.

ISBN: 978-1-6655-3597-7 (sc)
978-1-6655-3596-0 (e)

Print information available on the last page.

Published by AuthorHouse  08/25/2021

authorHOUSE®

# TABLE OF CONTENTS

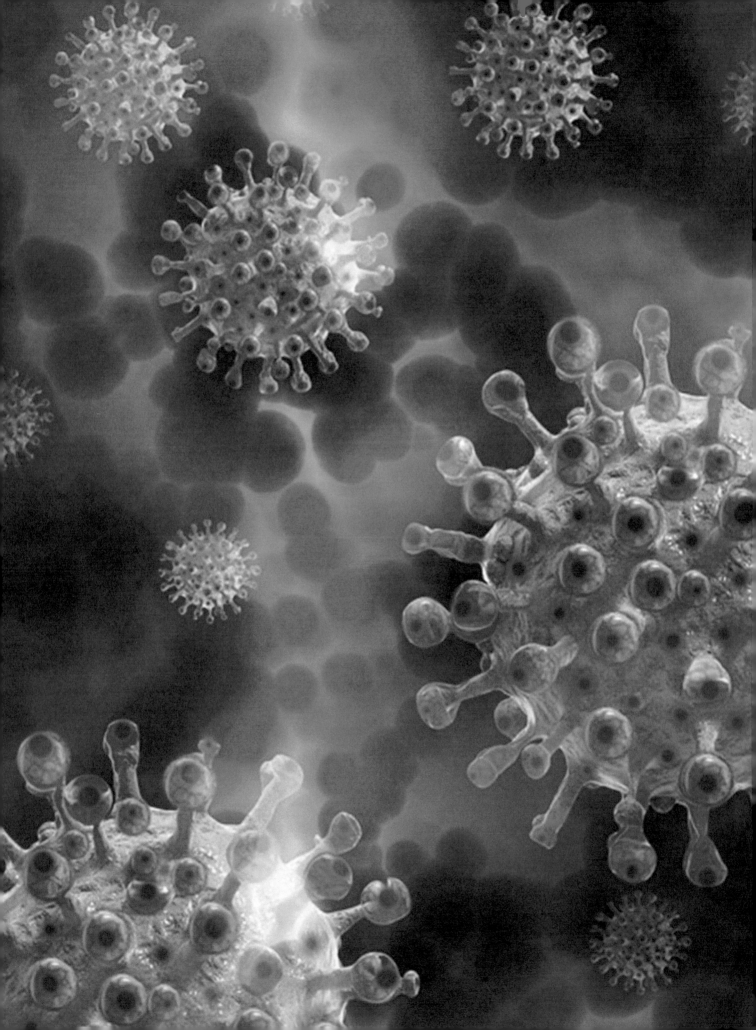

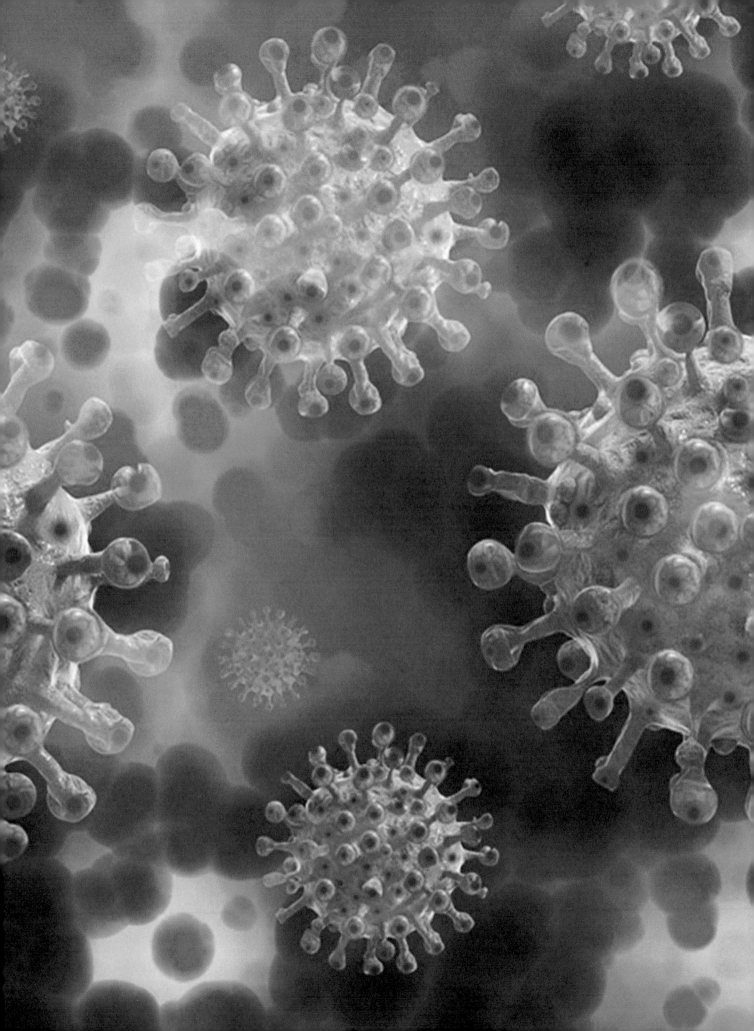

# CHAPTER ONE

# TRUE COVID 19 IN 2020
# WHO IS CORONA?  WHAT IS CORONA?

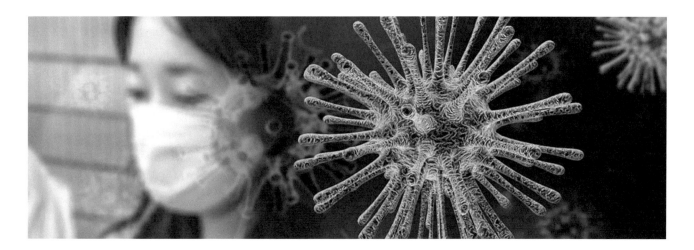

"One of the ways it can do that good international citizen and providing all this aid to other countries who are now entering really tough times with this virus and Beijing will reap political rewards from that." The Chinese government has had an ongoing credibility problem with its own citizens since the outbreak unfold. Authorities have been forced to Monitor Chinese Social Media sites to remove floods of angry comments criticizing the government's handling of the outbreak which was initially deemed delayed and reckless. Authorities actively suppressed information at the virus ' outset and silenced those who attempted to speak out about it, prompting global condemnation of the Chinese communist party. But that a side, this also ties into Mr. Xi's long -running vision of placing China at the center of the world. There are two important trends playing our right now: the United States is focusing in ward, and Donald Trump- Dr. Davis says- is clearly clueless about how to hand le this crisis ." At the same time, he says Mr. Xi wants to use the pandemic to present China as a benevolent global leader who is stepping into the leadership vacuum that the US left behind. But at the end of the day, China will expect their assistance will become with benefits, and will expect states to pay tribute to China in the form of acquiescing to China's interests in other areas . There are big geopolitical strings attached to the other side no matter what. " If the US severely weakened, in terms of long-term economic damage, the Chinese will be tempted to extend in that situation to their benefit. We could see China not only trying to use soft power and the perception of being a provide of economic goods to try to win global leadership, but also to resolve some issues with hard power.'' In particular, he suggests all eyes should be on Taiwan once the pandemic is behind us .'' I think that if the Chinese felt that if the US simply wasn't able to respond, because move against Taiwan . If the US couldn't come to Taiwan's assistance, then this would future erode US credibility in the eyes of the region. Coronavirus origin: Where did Covid-19 come from? San Francisco- The novel Coronavirus was first discovered in China and it rapidly spread around the globe. But where did it come from? " Based on everything that scientists have looked at of the genetic material of this Coronavirus, the similarity is closest to a virus in a bat, '' said ABC7 News Special Correspondent Dr. Alok Patel, a member of our team of Coronavirus experts. Scientists believe a bat likely infected another animal before it infected humans. The intermediary animal is still a mystery but some scientists suspect it's likely a scaly mammal called a pangolin . " Then t h e virus evolved. It changed form and it became ready to infect humans at a large scale, " said Dr. Patel. How it got to humans is still unknown. Scientists is are still trying to figure it out right now, as well as trying to figure out where exactly that animal origin is because understanding this could help us understand the next p an d emic," said Dr. Patel. The novel Coronavirus is a zoonotic disease, meaning an infection that can jump bet ween different species . "Both SAR S and MERS are examples of viruses that came from mother nature'' said Dr. Pate l. " In the case of SARS, scientists believe the virus came from a bat then went to a civet cat, and then infected humans. In the case of MERS, they believe the intermediary animal was a camel .'' Humans been fighting off zoonotic disease forever. '' Now the World Health Organization estimates that 60% of all human pathogens have a zoonotic origin,'' said Dr. Patel. " You might be saying I've never heard of a zoonotic disease, yes you have. Because of rabies, salmonella, West Nile Virus, Ebola, and Coronavirus, this one, are all examples of zoonotic diseases cause a mild illness while others can spread quickly, infecting, and potentially causing a lot death. Sometimes a disease shows up and our immunes systems have never seen it before, making it difficult for our bodies to fight it off. There are many ways for zoonotic diseases to be passed around. Animal to person, to person, in food, even in water. Even the flu is a zoonotic virus . "

We suspect the 1918 flu was an avian flu,'' said Dr Patel. The 1918 flu pandemic is believed to have killed 50 million people and infected a third of the global population at the time. Though it was called the Spanish flu, researchers now believe it started in the U.S., on a pig farm in Kansas.

Here's what some experts believe happened : A bird with the flu and human with a common seasonal flu infected a pig. The two flus mutated in a pig and created a new virus. Now the reason the 1918 flu was so deadly, similar to this Coronavirus, is because humans had no immunity against it,' ' s aid Dr Patel . That's why understanding where the novel Coronavirus came from is key to understanding how we got it. One clue might be in those spiky proteins that allow the virus to infect you. And these specific proteins work dangerously well and have never been seen before." This is important, this is why every single major scientific journal and authority believe that the virus came from nature, and not a lab,'' said Dr Patel. Where did the 38,000 Covid-19 recoveries' come from? Here's DOH 's explanation Manila- on top of the record- high 3,954 additional Covid-19 cases reported on Thursday, people were surprised by the Department of Health 's (DOH) announcement of an additional 38,075 recovered patients. As of Thursday, there are 65,064 patient in the Philippines who have recovered from Covid-19, according to the DOH. Read: PH logs record-high 38 K add '1 recoveries, 3,954 new Covid-19 cases This is even higher than the previous count of total recoveries at 26,996 on Wednesday. As of Thursday, there are 65,064 patients in the Philippines who have recovered from Covid-19, according to the DOH. The department first mentioned its data reconciliation efforts with local units in mid- July, with its reports showing a spike in the number of cases, deaths, and recoveries. Even before that, the numbers being released by local government units were different from The DOH Because of delayed reporting. Read: Philippines records 2,124 new Covid-19 cases; recoveries, deaths sike. The DOH addressed this by using a digital platform called Covid Kaya, which allowed hospitals and laboratories to directly in put their data into a central data base. The DOH explained that of the 38,075 additional recoveries, 909 are from the regular reporting of their epidemiological surveillance units and 37,166 are from OPLan recovery,'' Which is an initiative that the Department activated to monitor the statuses of confirmed Covid-19 cases .'' These 37,166 patients were re-tagged as recoveries after LGU and regional centers of Health Development personnel rechecked their status a DOH staff told ABS-CBN news. " Early this month the DOH created the Covid-19 surveillance and Quick Action unit which focuses on data collection validation, and reconciliation of information available at the local and national level, through the Covid Kaya platform,'' the DOH said in its statement. The DOH said it made a " mass recovery adjustment'' by reclassifying mild and a symptomatic cases, which resulted in around 5,000 additional recoveries earlier this month. Back in June, DOH explained that their updated guidelines no longer require Covid-19 patients to under go repeat testing in order to be released from the hospital. The DOH said patients only need medial assessment by their doctor, showing that they have not had any symptoms in the last 3 days and that they have completed their 14-day quarantine. Read: Updated Covid-19 testing guidelines include Jail personnel, social workers, other front liners Department Memorandum No.2020-0258 States that patients with mild or no symptoms are tagged as recovered 14 days from the date of onset of symptoms or by date of specimen collection, the DOH said " Current recovery policies now show that at the 10$^{th}$ day illness, the risk of transmitting the virus to other people is significantly reduced, the DOH said, adding that the same Protocol is followed by the US CDC, European CDC, and India. Those who a symptomatic are still required to follow a 14-day isolation period ." Up on assessment of a licensed physician the patient can be tagged as recovered after completion of 14-days isolation period,'' it added . The DOH also said that '' data on recovery reconciliations will be reported every 15 days .'' This means that there might be a spike in the number of recoveries every 15 days. At 85,486, Coronavirus infections in PH surpass main land China's tally Read more: Covid -19 Coronavirus Covid-19 cases in the Philippines Covid-19 recoveries Coronavirus patients Covid-19 recovered patients in Philippines. What is coronavirus? The different types What is coronavirus? Coronaviruses are family of virus that cause illness in humans and animals . Seven different types have been found in people, including those responsible for the SARS MERS and Covid-19 pandemics. Early reports suggest the new virus is more contagious than the one causing SARS but less likely to cause severe symptoms. There is much we need to learn about the new Coronavirus (Covid-19). What are the types of Coronavirus? Coronaviruses (covs) are a family of viruses that cause respiratory and intestinal illnesses in humans and animals. They usually cause mild colds in people but the emergence of the severe acute respiratory syndrome (SARS) epidemic in China in 2002-2003 and the Middle East respiratory Syndrome (MERS) on the Arabian Peninsula in 2012 show they can also cause severe disease. Since December 2019, the world has been battling another Coronavirus. Severe acute respiratory syndrome Coronavirus 2 (SARS – cov-2) is the virus responsible for the current outbreak of Coronavirus disease (Covid-19), Which was first identified in Wuhan, China, following reports of serious pneumonia. [2] [3] What do Coronaviruses look like? Coronaviruses are relatively simple structures, and then- from helps us to understand how they work. They are spherical and coated with spikes of protein. These spikes help the virus bind to and infect healthy cells. However, the same spikes are also what allows the immune system to see ' the virus. Bits of the spike can be used in potential Coronavirus vaccines to prompt the body to produce anti-bodies against this new virus. They are named for the distinctive appearance of their spikes; When seen under a powerful microscope, the spikes look like a crown (Corona is the Latin for crown). Beneath these spikes is a layer of membrane. This membrane can be disrupted by detergents and alcohols, which is why soap and water and alcohol hand sanitizer gels are effective against the virus. Inside the membrane is the virus ' genetic material - its genome.

Where as the genomes of some viruses like chicken box and small box are made of DNA like humans, those of Coronaviruses are made of the closely related RNA. RNA viruses have small genomes which are subject to constant change. These changes, called Mutations, help the virus adapt to and infect new host species. It is though that the new Covid-19 likely originated from bats but it is not yet known whether Mutations allowed this jump from animals to humans. [4] What is different about the new Coronavirus? The new SARS- cov-2, is most closely related to a group of SARS- covs found in humans, bats, pangolins and civets. Even though there are many similarities between the new Covid-19 and the virus that caused the SARS epidemic, there are also differences resulting from changes in their genomes. This includes how they are passed from one individual to another, and the differing symptoms of Coronaviruses. Early reports suggest that the new Coronavirus is more contagious than the virus that caused SARS but less likely to cause severe disease. How many Coronaviruses are found in humans? To date seven human Coronaviruses (H covs) have been identified (see table below).

[1]5] Four of them are common; less high risk and typically cause only mild respiratory illness in healthy human adults. However, they contribute to a third of common cold infections and, in higher risk people with weak immue systems, they can cause long term, life threatening illnesses. The other three (those causing MES, SARS and Covid-19 cases) are known to cause more severe illness such as shortness of breath and even death. Covid-19 illness tends to be, milder than SARS and MERS but more severe than disease caused by four common Coronaviruses. Human Coronavirus name SARS -cov-2 SARS-cov MERS-cov Hcov-NL63 Hcov-229E Hcov-OC43 HKUL Illness Covid-19 severe acute respiratory syndrome (SARS) Middle East respiratory syndrome (MERS) Usually mild respiratory illness Because this virus is new, no-one has any immunity to it. This means it will potentially infect very large numbers of people. And even though the number of very severe cases is low in percentage terms a small percentage of a very large number adds up to many people with acute illness. It is though that all seven human Coronaviruses might have been transmitted to humans from other animals. Those causing MERS, SARS and Covid-19 from probably originated from bats. Its is possible that the transfer of the new Covid-19 from its original host species to humans involved another animal species, such as the pangolin as an intermediate host. coronavirus- Wikipedia Coronaviruses are a group of related RNA viruses that cause diseases in mammals and birds. In humans and birds they cause respiratory tract infections that can range from mild to lethal. Mild illnesses in humans include some cases of the common cold (which is also caused by other viruses, predominantly rhinoviruses), while more lethal varieties can cause SARS, MERS, and Covid-19.

Where Coronaviruses come from and why we haven 't eradicated them: Bats appear to be the source of the coronavirus, but it's not yet clear which types, of animals, were the'' intermediate hosts'' that jump from animals to humans. Buts are especially notorious for hosting a number of harmful viruses in the past including SARS, MERS, and Ebola . It's unclear where the novel Coronavirus comes from but researches have considered bats and pangolins as possible source. Most humans have already been infected with some strain of Coronavirus, experts say, but it's unlikely the illness was as severe as certain cases of Covid-19. With the world focused on the novel Coronavirus, SARS- Cov-2, spreading around the world and claiming tens of thousands of lives as of this writing it's part of a broader collection of Coronaviruses. And those Coronaviruses are group of viruses that cause a wide range of illnesses, most of    which lead to upper respiratory infections, said    JacquelineVernarelli, PhD, sacred Health University director of research education and an assistant professor of public health. Coronaviruses: Coronaviruses are a large group of viruses that cause diseases in animals and humans. They of ten circulate among camels, cats, and bats, and can sometimes evolve and infect people. In animals, Coronaviruses can cause diarrhea in cows and pigs, and upper respiratory disease in chickens. In humans, the viruses can cause mild respiratory infections, like the common cold but can lead to serious illnesses, like pneumonia. Coronaviruses are named for crown- like spikes on their surface. Human Coronaviruses were first identified in the mild-1960 's. They are closely monitored by public health officials. Novel Coronavirus (Covid-19) A novel Coronavirus (SARS-cov-2) that causes the disease Coronavirus Disease 2019 (Covid-19) emerged in a seafood and poultry market in the Chinese city of Wuhan in2019. Cases have been detected worldwide, and on March11,2020 the World Health Organization characterized the outbreak as a pandemic Human-to – Human transmission occurs through close contract. Middle East Respiratory Syndrome (MERS) was first reported in 2012 in Saudi Arabia and spread to more than 25 other countries. MERS originated in camels and emerged to infect people. Symptoms usually include fever, cough, and shortness of breath, and often progress to pneumonia. About 3or4 out of every 10 patients reported with MERS have died. MERS cases continue to occur, primarily in the Arabian peninsula; however, as of 2019, there have been only two confirmed cases of MERS in the US, both in 2014. Severe Acute Respiratory Syndrome (SARS) Severe Acute Respiratory syndrome (SARS) originated in small mammal and emerged to infect people. SARS was first reported in Southern China in 2002 and the illness spread to more than two dozen countries in North America, South America, Europe, and Asia. Symptoms include fever, chills, and body aches, and may progress to pneumonia. Infection with the SARS virus causes acute respiratory distress (severe breathing difficulty), with a mortality rate of about 10 percent. No human cases of SARS True Covid19 in 2020

# CHAPTER TWO

# TRUE COVID 19 IN 2020
# WHO IS CORONA? WHAT IS CORONA?

**H**ave been reported any where in the world since2004. Symptoms: Most people get infected with human strains of Coronaviruses a some point in their lives. These illnesses usually last for a short amount of time, and Symptoms may include: .fever .cough .headache .runny nose . sore throat Additional symptoms have been reported with Covid-19. Human Coronaviruses can cause other more serious illnesses, such as pneumonia or bronchitis. This is more common in individuals with heart and lung disease, those with weakened immune systems, infants, and older adults. If you are concerned about symptoms, call a health care professional and tell them about recent travel or exposures. Do not go directly to the doctor's office or hospital, where you may infect other people. Diagnosis: There are laboratory tests to detect human coronaviruses. For Covid-19, viral tests can detect current infection, and anti-body test can detect past infection. If you think you may have a Coronavirus, talk to a health care professional. Prevention: .coughing and sneezing .close personal contact(within about 6 feet,) such as touching or shaking hands, touching your month, nose, or eyes, fecal contamination (rarely) There are currently no vaccines available to protect against many Coronaviruses, but clinical trials are underway to develop vaccines for Covid-19. There are steps you can take to help prevent infection: wash your hands often with soap and water for at least 20 seconds avoid touching your eyes, nose, or mouth cover your mouth and nose when you cough or sneeze .clean and surfaces .avoid close contact with people who are sick and stay home while you are sick: Treatment: There is currently no specific treatment for Coronaviruses in general, other than good supportive care: .Take pain and fever medications .use a humidifier or take a hot shower .drink plenty of liquids .stay home and rest many clinical trials are underway in the United States and other countries to evaluate new drugs for treating patients with Covid-19. Updated August 2020 source: Center for disease control and prevention common Questions and answers about Covid-19 for older adults and people with Chronic Health Conditions: The National Foundation for infectious Diseases and the Alliance for Aging Research developed this resource on Covid-19 for older adults and people with underlying health conditions. Is china growing these coronaviruses plants to harvest for what is it for to make coronaviruses to kill thousands of people in the United States? How many of these killer coronaviruses plants that china has in the fields is the coronaviruses plants grows like cotton in the fields? China labs is making the coronaviruses and what type of chemicals are they putting in the coronaviruses to make people ill and sick and died? How long does it take for the poison killer coronaviruses to have effect on humans and how long that these patients have to suffer before they died from the killer poison coronaviruses that china grow and shipped to the United States is president Donald Trump really involved in with china by bring in this killer coronaviruses into the United States like Washington D.C. and New York that was hit hard in 2020. Now are the United States ready for a change in the nation people such as a new president of the United States of America are you American people ready for that change is coming to the United States so the other thousands and thousands of American peoples of all colors of races peoples White American people and Black American people in the United State of American are you ready to vote for a new president of the United States and a new Republican parties and new Democrats parties as well to change the old ways of the presidential election to positive and change to a new vice president too. The change have come now for the nation to vote for the new president of the United States of America. People of the nation wake up to a brighter days to come in the 2020 Election in Nov. Election. Just stay prayed up through the o mighty god the lord Jesus Christ our savior to the Amen! God is good all the time peoples the battle is not yours it the Lords believe that American peoples of all colors of races that including White Americans and Black Americans peoples. All Lives Matters in this World and on this earth. God created the Haven and the Earth. God send his forgotten son Jesus Christ down to wash away all sin away peoples amen! So peoples of all colors of races White American people and Black American people stop the violence end this right now cause god don't like ugly and he is very mad of you peoples of all colors of races including the poor White American people and the poor Black American people stop the killing stop destroy thin g that don 't b el on g to you Black Americans peoples get you a Job get a Education a go the trade school learn how to do things with your minds. And stop killing and rubbering steeling out the communities. All Lives does Matters peoples. Not just Blacks Not just Whites and any other that including colors of races of peoples all this stupid foolish crazy thing doesn't mount to nothing it's bull mess peoples think hard about what you doing and who are you peoples hurting you really hurting your selves indeed you are. When is this going to stop? The coronavirus covid-19 and this bull mess that China brought into the United States is called Coronavirus Pandemic and the Killer Coronaviruses that kills. This Coronaviruses come from China and Donald Trump and the U.S. Government and the Governor of China all involved in the deaths of thousands of peoples of the United States of America in 2020 is the History of the Covid-19 Coronavirus Pandemic Crisis! Peoples the Coronaviruses come from a seed and the seed is planted into the fields in China it's not grown here in the United States. Covid-19 cases have gone down, but fight not over yet ': Delhi CM Kejriwal: Delhi CM Arvind Kejriwal pointed out that in past one month, cases of Covid-19 have gone down, deaths have reduced, recovery rate has increased and positivity ratio has lowered. Delhi chief minister Arvind Kejriwal on Saturday said the two crore people of city, his government and the centre have together attained victory in controlling Covid-19 but the fight is not over yet.

Speaking virtually at the inauguration of 450- bed Delhi government hospital in Burari, he said Covid-related parameters have improved in Delhi in the last one month . " The two crore Delhi people Del h i government and centre have together attained victory over Corona but it would not be correct to say that the fight is over," he said. The chief minister pointed out that in past one month, cases of Covid-19 have gone down, deaths have reduced and positivity radio has lowered. This is a result of the hard work of all the people. I want to congratulate all the doctors, nurses, paramedic staff, officials, and whoever has worked hard to achieve this goal.'' He said the Burari hospital will increase the number of beds for Coronavirus patients in the city.

"I am very happy to be inaugurating Burari hospital today. I could not be there due to Covid-19 and various other arrangements. The opening of this hospital will add 450 more beds in the health infrastructure in Delhi," Kejriwal said . Health Minister Satyendar Jan inaugurated the hospital and was joined through video conferencing by the chief minister. The hospital will eventually have a total of 700 beds. Around125 beds will have oxygen supply and the capacity will be enhanced in the coming days, the Delhi government said in a statement. Extend deadline for new five safety norms till March 2021: Hotel owners As hotels and guest houses in the capital gear up to reopen after a lull of five months, owners of such establishments have a new reason to worry- a bunch of new fire safety norms, which were notified in May2019.

The owners have requested the Delhi government to extend the deadline (from March31,2020 to March31,2021) for implementation of new norms that are currently under view Adelegation of Delhi Hotel an d Restaurant owner's Association met chief minister Arvind Kejriwal in this regard on Friday. The new rules demand amendments to building by laws to strengthen fire safety norms. As per the Commented news amendments, kitchen or cooking activity in any form is not allowed on roof tops or basements of buildings, and storage of inflammable materials or temporary roofing is banned in terraces. Besides, inflammable materials- like carpets and wooden or foam pane lings- are not allowed on passages, corridors and stair cases of buildings, and storage of gas cylinders in violation of standards prescribed by the National Building code is also banned. After a massive fi re in Karol Bach 's Hotel Arp it Palace claimed 17 lives in February last year, the Delhi government had got all hotels in Paharganj and Karol Bagh inspected. The government had later notified amendments to the building by laws to strengthen fire safety norms in May 2019. The amendments, which are under review after hotel owners raised concerns about certain provisions, were to be implemented by December 2019 but was extended till March 31, 2020. In November last year, the Delhi government had constituted a sub- committee, which was chaired by a special commissioner of police (licensing), to review and make appropriate recommendations for five safety of guest houses and restaurants. The committee is yet to submit it's report said a senior police official. Mohit Shah, general secretary of Delhi Hotel and Restaurant Owner's Association, said," The process got delayed due to the pandemic. Our fire no cs not valid right now since the new norms were notified. After the recommendations of the committee are notified we need time to implement the new fire safety norms. In our meeting with the with the CM on Friday, were quested him to extend the deadline for the 'implementation of the norms till March 31, 202 1.'' On Friday, the Delhi Fire

Service held a meeting with the Delhi government's principal secretary (home) to decide on the issue. A meeting with chief secretary Vijay Dev was also held recently to discuss the matter, said a senior official, requesting anonymity. According to a senior of financial in the home department of 'Delhi government, the decision to extend the deadline for the implementation of the new norms has to be taken by the urban development department." So far no decision has been taken in this regard, '' said a senior official with the urban development department.'' Hotel owners say that they need time till next ear, as the industry is badly hit due to the pandemic and there is shortage of labourers." Implementation of the new norms require some changes in our building. But right now, construction workers are not easily available. Moreover, we want to first restart our businesses,'' said Boddy Lohia, president of Mahipalpur hotel owner's Association. The hotel owners had raised objections to a few provisions in the amendment, such as installation of carbon monoxide detectors and fire check or protection doors, and no fire no cs to hotels with more than four floors. Former DFS chief Ak Sharma said the new amendments were an outcome of the Hotel Arpit Palace fire tragedy as it was realized that these hotels need additional norms with respect to life and fire safety. He said that the new norms should be implemented in a time bound manner." Not only in view of the Covid-19 pandemic, but even earlier also these hotel owner organizations had requested. Time for implement these mandates. Are we not playing with the safety of people? Since the government has decided to open hotels, there view committee should get it done on war footing and the report must be submitted with out delay. The same must be implemented in a time bound manner. Thereafter, those who do not implement the new rules must be penalized,'' Sharma said. Every hotel or a lodging house needs a license from DCP (licensing) to run it, under the Delhi police act. For obtaining the license, an application form has to be accompanied with land ownership proof, rent agreement and the site and building plan and the premise has to be inspected by the licensing branch. Joint commissioner of police (licensing) sur as his Choudhary said the report is being prepared by the sub- committee can d is expected to be submitted within the next two weeks ." T h e new rules issued by the fire department through a notification dated May 27, 2019, were not being followed by many hotel owners also had apprehensions towards the new norms, the committee was then set up in November last year to review them,'' Choudhary said . Delhi police's public relations officer Eish Singhal also did. Not comment on the matter. A Delhi government spokesperson s aid," The government will consider their proposal and decide after examining all the details. Kejriwal urges centre to restart metro services in city: Delhi chief minister Arvind Kejriwal on Sunday said that he has urged the central government to consider restarting metro services in the city in a phased manner if needed, and conduct a trial run regarding the same soon . " People of Delhi have been requesting us to start metro services. We have taken this up with the central government on several occasions. We have urged the centre to explore the possibility of resuming metro services in Delhi, while keeping it prohibited in other states as of now. Delhi is a special cases because we have the Covid-19 situation under control,'' said Kej riwal in a speech at the end of a webinar with trades in th e city. De lhi Metro R ail Corpo ratio n 's services have been shut since March 22 (Janata cur few). With nearly six million passenger journeys daily the metro is the lifeline of Delhi. Though Metro services are closed the centre and the Delhi government allowed buses and para-transit modes to operate, with restrictions on number of passengers, since May. According to transport officials, currently there are close to 6,500 buses plying on Delhi roads. With a majority of the services reopened since June, when the centre announced unlock 1, people of Delhi continue to face inconveniences while commuting and mostly have to rely on their personal vehicles. Kejriwal s aid," We have urged the centre to consider a phased approach for resuming metro services if needed. They can at least conduct trial runs on a experimental basis '' The decision to res tart metro services can be taken by the Union Ministry of home affairs. Meanwhile, the DMRC and the central Industrial security force (CISF), which is in- change of security, have prepared protocols to ensure smooth and contactless travel for passengers inside stations and a trains. The two agencies have drafted rules that focus on the need to ensure social distancing at metro stations and in trains once the centre allows operations to begin. Completely cashless True Covid19 in 2020 CHAPTER THREE Who is Corona? What is Corona?

The True Covid-19 Coronavirus. transaction at ticketing counters, earmarking designated spots for passengers to stand while waiting for trains or at ticketing counters, use of face masks and Arogya set up mobile application, leaving alternate seats vacant are some of the measures that metro has decided to take once the service resume. Anuj Dayal executive director, corporate communication DMR C, said '' The DMRC shall be prepared to commence operations when ever directed by the government. All necessary guidelines to combat the spread of Covid-19 shall be implemented and all efforts shall be made to make travel safe for our commuters .'' The metro recently launched its new smart card to promote cashless transactions and also ensure contact less travel. The smart card has an automatic top-up facility. The cards will be available to commuters once the metro gets a go-ahead to resume its operations. According to senior metro officials, the smart cards will automatically be recharged at the Automatic Fare collection (AFC) entry gates with Rs 200 when ever the balance goes below Rs 100. These measures are based on the guidelines provided by the Union Ministry of Housing and urban affairs to all metro corporations in the country for drafting standard operating procedures. HI had recently reported that the CISF has also started preparations for the resumption of metro services in Delhi – NCR. According to officials, they been asked to mobilise staff, set up equipment and ensure that all required precautionary measures are in place to resume train service on a short notice. The CISF has also prepared its own SOPS, which includes use of the Aarogya setu app to identify Covid-19 patients. CISF personnel, who come in direct contact with travellers at metro stations, will be required to sanitize their hands after every two or three travellers. New Research: Bats Harbor hundreds of Coronaviruses, and s p ill overs aren 't rare Three years ago, NPR accompanied disease ecologist Kevin Olival on a field trip to Malaysian Borneo. Olival, who is with the nonprofit research group Eco Health Alliance, was there to trap bats and collect samples for viruses. Bats are known for carrying some dangerous ones Particularly viruses that have the potential to kick off global out breaks through what' s called " spillovers '' - instances of an animal virus jumping into a human. So there searches were on a hunt for the next big threat. The results of their work put the current Coronavirus out break in China in a wholly new light. Scientists say it was caused by a spillover event. And the findings from the sample collection project suggest these kinds of spillovers have actually been quietly taking place in China for years. Swabbing Bats: The evidence comes from hours of pain staking sample collection sessions, like the one NPR with nessed in Borneo: Olival is at the edge of a rain forest, sitting in a make shift out door lab. There are plastic chairs. On a folding table, he places a small female b at. " It's ok,

girl. It's ok, girl,'' s ays Oliva l s ooth in gly as

th e bat wriggles . '' So we're ge ttin g th e oral

s wab in th e bac k o f the throat,'' Ol iva l

exp lai ns ." An d I'm ju s t h old ing her h ead

b et wee n my two fi n gers .'' He s miles ."

Oo oh, good o n e! Th ere's d efi n itel y s ome

s amp le on th at s wab . " T h e bat give s a

sudden squ ea k." T h at was a react in g to a

recta l s wab,'' says Ol ival wryly. A f ew more

s wab s an d it's all d on e. " Now sh e ge ts h er

s p ec ial treat,'' says Olival." A little bit of Mango juice as are ward .'' At that time, Olival and his colleagues were also in the process of collecting samples from thousands of bats in China. Fast forward to the present day. Olival says what they found is alarming: '' We found evidence for, in total, from all the sampling we did in China, about 400 new strains of Coronaviruses .'' That means 400 potential candidates to spark another outbreak in China back in 2002- severe acute respiratory syndrome, or SARS. And this current outbreak is from a SARS- related Coronavirus.

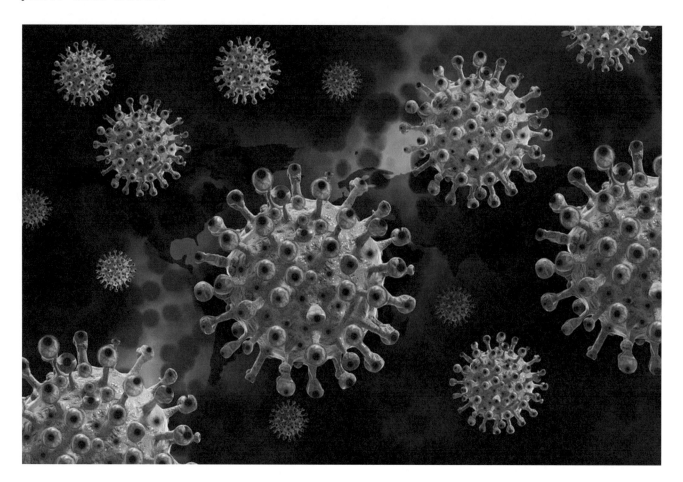

A direct path to humans It worse: Scientists had though spillovers were rare- that bat Coronaviruses weren 't generally capable of infecting humans, so it took complicated steps. Steps one: A bat Coronavirus would have to infect some animal species that had closer contact with people than bats do. Step two: While in that other animal' s bod y, the virus would need to pick up new genetic code. But the sampling project found that those steps are not needed, says Olival." What we showed was that SARS- related viruses in these bat populations have the potential to go directly into need that extral, mutational step [of] infecting another host.'' In other words, the path to sparking new out breaks is potentially much more direct. For example, one of the Coronaviruses that the researchers found was a very close genetic match for the SARS virus. So they put it in a petridish with human cells. The virus succeeded in infecting the cells. Bat contact Olival says the fact that a bat Coronavirus had at least this biological ability in a lab setting raised an obvious next question: Is there evidence infecting people in the real world? So the researchers started talking blood samples from villagers in China who lived near some of the bat caves they'd been studying. Hongying Li is an ecologist with Eco Health Alliance. She says there any number of ways these people seemed at risk of in advertently coming into contact with bat saliva, urine or poop .'' In some places you could find bats roosting in people's homes,'' she says .'' And people even visited the bat caves, says Li. The caves were a particularly popular hang out in the summer, when they provided respite from the heat.'' W hen we wen t to the caves for sampling we'd usually see people's beer bottles and water bottles,'' says Li. She and her colleagues checked the villagers ' blood for signs of recent infections with bat Coronaviruses. The team did this again with people in some other rural areas. Each time, says Li,'' we found Coronaviruses that had already spilled over into the human population .'' These were multiple mini -out breaks that had gone undetected. Olival says this discovery was a huge red flag: " The signal is there that these SARS-related viruses were jumping into people even if they weren't causing any noticeable di ease.'' Indeed, people might have even had symptoms, but health authorities simply never picked up on it. Spillovers: Which brings us to this current Coronavirus outbreak. As soon as it started, Eco Health Alliance's long time collaborators in china 1 principally researchers at Wuhan Institute of virology and the Wuhan Jinyintan Hospital) compared the new virus with the bat samples they'd collected . ' They found an extremely close match . " A viral taxonomist would probably call that the same virus species,'' says Olival. That suggests this current outbreak-which has infected tens of thousands of people-could have come directly from bats, says Olival. And, he adds, the larger take away is clear: " These bat SAR S -related Coronaviruses are actively spilling over in the human p op u lati on .'' Not all of them will s p ark deadly pandemics. But the more frequent these spillovers, the greater the changes. Fact check: Early research shows fabric could neutralize Coronaviruses. Corrections & clarifications: This story has been updated to clarify the development of this type of fabric dates back to 2005, when it was patented by Jeffry Skiba and Lawrence Schneider. Claim: Researchers found a fabric that kills Coronaviruses ' T here's reason to be skeptical of any internet post claiming something kills the Coronavirus. Facebook in particular can be a deluge of home remedies that range from unproven to downright dangerous. What you really need to know about Coronavirus? The coronavirus epidemic is shaking up public health authorities around the world-but what does it mean for you? To protect yourself and your family, while keeping your risk in perspective, here's the latest information and answers to common question on Coronavirus: what is Coronavirus? Coronaviruses are a group of viruses that cause disease in both animals and humans. They're named for the distinctive crown-like spikes on the virus surface. Human Coronaviruses were identified decades ago, in the mid-1960s. The virus typically cause mid cases of the common cold but can lead to respiratory infections like pneumonia. The name of the current Coronavirus is " severe acute respiratory syndrome Coronavirus 2,' ' or SaRS-Cov-2. Is Coronavirus contagious? The current form of Coronavirus disease, officially known as Covid-19 (Covid-19 is the name of the disease, and SARS-cov-2 is the name of the virus that cause it), was first reported in late December 2019 in Wuhan, China. By February's end, 50 countries experienced cases of Coronavirus disease. An outbreak among more than 700 passengers and crew members of the Diamond Princess cruise ship docked to a temporary quarantine, shows how efficiently the virus can spread-the out- break started with one passenger who'd been traveling from china. An outbreak in a Kirkland, Washington, nursing home is another example of the virus spreading among people living together in close quarters. This weekend, the nursing home was locked down after four more cases were confirmed. How does Coronavirus spread? Covid-19 appears to spread primarily through droplets as the infected person coughs or sneezes. These respiratory droplets either land in the mouths or noses of people nearby, or may be in haled. However the virus has also been found in blood and stool, which raises questions about other possible routes of transmission according to a commentary published Feb.28th in the journal Jama.

# CHAPTER THREE

# TRUE COVID 19 IN 2020
# WHO IS CORONA?  WHAT IS CORONA?

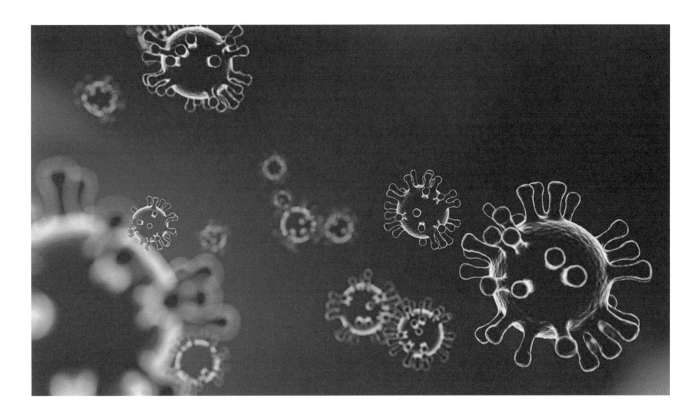

U.S. Intelligence confirms China Is Responsible for spreading disinformation
In United States about Coronavirus       Six us intelligence agencies confirmed Chinese operatives help push viral fraudulent text messages containing disinformation about the federal government's response, to Wuhan coronavirus crisis, according to a new report from the New York Times. The fake text messages, which were widely shared false information claiming the Trump administration was instituting a country-wide lockdown with the help of the national guard. " This is real, I just got this report. Homeland security is preparing to mobilize the national guard. Preparing to dispatch them across the us along with military. They will also call on first responders,'' the text messages read .'' They are preparing to announce a

nationwide two week quarantine for all citizens. All businesses closed . Everyone at home.'' The messages were so wide spread, the White House National Security Council put out a statement telling Americans the rumors were false. " Text message rumors of a national quarantine are fake. There is no national lockdown. The CDC has and will continue to post the latest guidance on Covid-19 .'' The White House tweeted . There is no national lockdown.@ CDC gov has and will continue to post the latest guidance on # Covid-19.

# CHAPTER FOUR

# TRUE COVID 19 IN 2020
# WHO IS CORONA? WHAT IS CORONA?

Coronavirus: when will the outbreak end and life get back to normal? The world is shutting down. Places that were once teeming with the hustle and bustle of daily life have become ghost-towns with massive restrictions put on our lives-from lockdowns and school closures to travel restrictions and bans on mass gatherings. It is an unparalleled global response to a disease. But when will it end and when will we be able to get on with our lives? Prime Minister Boris Johnson has said he believes the UK can " turn the tide'' against the outbreak within the next 12 weeks and the country can "send Coronavirus packing.'' But even if the number of cases starts to fall in the next three months, then we will still be far from the end. It can taken along time for the tide to go out-possibly years. It is clear the current strategy of shutting down large parts of society is not sustainable in the long-term. The social and economic damage would be catastrophic. What countries need is an " exit strategy" - a way of lifting the restrictions and getting back to normal. But the Coronavirus is not going to disappear. It you lift the restrictions that are holding the virus back, then cases will inevitably soar." We do have a big problem in what the exit strategy is and how we get out of this," says mark wool house, a professor of infectious disease epidemiology at the University of Edinburgh. " It's not just the UK no country has an exit strategy." It is a massive scientific and societal challenge. More about Coronavirus .A simple Grid: What are the symptoms? . New Guidance : what must I do? . New Restrictions: what are they? . Look-up Tool: Check cases in your area . Maps and Charts: Visual guide to the outbreak There are essentially three ways out of this mess. . Vaccination . enough people develop immunity through infection or permanently chance, our behaviour1 society Each of these routes would reduce the ability of the virus to spread. Vaccines- at least 12-18 months away A vaccine should give some one immunity so they do not become sick if they are exposed. Immunize enough people, about 60% of the population, and the virus cannot cause, out-breaks- the concept known as herd immunity. The first person was given an experimental vaccine in the US this week after researchers were allowed to skip the usual rules of performing animals test first. Vaccine research is taking place at unprecedented speed, but there is no guarantee it will be successful and will require immunization on global scale. The best guess is along time to wait when facing unprecedented social restrictions during peace time . " Waiting for a vaccine should not be honoured with the name' strategy,' that is not a strategy" prof wool house told the BBC. Natural immunity- at least two years away the UK's short -term strategy is to drive down cases an much as possible to prevent hospitals being over whelmed when you run out of intensive care beds then deaths spike. Once cases are suppressed, it may allow some measure to be lifted for a while- unit cases rise and another round of restrictions are needed. When this might the be is uncertain . The UK's chief scientific advisor, sir Patrick Val lance, said " putting absolute time lines on things is not possible ." Doing this could, unintentionally, lead to herd immunity as more and more people were infected. But this could take years to build, up, according to Prof Neil Ferguson from Imperial College London : " We're talking about suppressing transmission at a level where by, hopefully, only a very small fraction of the country will be infected ." So eventually, if we continued this for two-plus years, may be a sufficient fraction of the country at that point might have been infected to give some degree of community protection ." But there is a question mark over whether this immunity will last. Other Coronaviruses, which cause common cold symptoms, lead to a very weak immune response and people can catch the same rise and another round of restrictions are needed. When this might be is uncertain The UK's chief scientific advisor, sir Patrick Vallance, said " putting absolute time lines on things is not possible ." Doing this could unintentionally, lead to herd immunity as more and more people were infected. But this could take years to build, up, according to Prof Neil Ferguson from Imperial College London :" We 're talking about suppressing transmission at a level where by, hopefully, only a very small fraction of the country will be infected ." So eventually, if we continued this for two- plus years, may be a sufficient fraction of the country at that point might have been infected to give some degree of community protection ." But there is a question mark over whether this immunity will last. Other Coronaviruses, which cause common cold symptoms, lead to a very weak immune response and people can catch same rise and another round or restrictions are needed . When this might be is said ' ' putting absolute time lines on things is not possible ." Doing this could unintentionally, lead to herd immunity as more and more people were infected. But this could take years to build, up, according to Prof Neil Ferguson From Imperial College London :'' We're talking about suppressing transmission at a level where by, hopefully, only a very small fraction of the country will be infected .'' So eventually, if we continued this two – plus years, may be a sufficient fraction of the country at that point might have been infected to give some degree of community protection .'' But there is a question mark over whether this immunity will last. Other Coronaviruses, which cause common cold symptoms, lead to a very weak immune response and people can catch the same bug multiple times in their life time. Coronavirus:

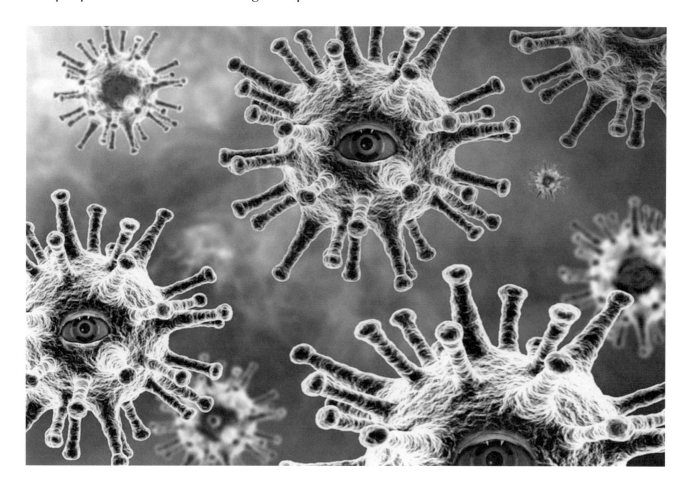

What you need to do is wash your hands Use a tissue for coughs Avoid touching your face Alternatives- no clear end point '' The third option is permanent changes in our behaviour that allow us to keep transmission rate s low,'' prof wool house said. This could include keeping some of the measures that have been put in place. Or introducing rigorous testing and isolation of patients to try to stay on top of any outbreaks.'' We did early detection and contact tracing the first time round and it d id n 't work.'' Prof wool hous e add s . Developing drugs that can successfully treat a Covid-19 infection could aid the other strategies too. They could be used as soon as people show symptoms in a process called '' transmission control'' to s top them passing it on to others. Or to treat patients in hospital to make the disease less deadly and reduce pressures on intensive care. This would have a similar effect by increasing the capacity to cope with larger outbreaks, I asked the UK's chief medical adviser, prof chris whitty, what his exit strategy was. He told me:'' Long term, clear a vaccine is one way out of this and we all hope that will happen as quickly as possible.'' And that'' globally, science will come up with solutions .'' 3 ways the Coronavirus could end Trump 's presidency voters are very influenced by what happens in an election year. The Coronavirus has quickly become a highly politicized election-year issue. Democrats have criticized president Trump for reacting slowly to the crisis, for contradicting the advise of his health experts and for spreading misinformation about the virus ." Trump h as counted b y accusing Democrats and the news media of exaggerating health risks to hurt his reelection campaign . T he American public 's views about the Coronavirus are polarized along partisan lines as well. Democrats were more than three times as likely to be '' very concerned '' about the virus than Republicans in the latest you Gov- economist poll (43 percent to 12 percent, respectively). Twice as many Democrats as Republicans said the Corona virus poses an " imminent threat" in a recent Ipsos – Reuters survey. It's not surprising that Republican s are minimizing the Coronavirus threat. Political science research highlights three ways that a pandemic could undermine support for president. Op-Ed: The Recession isn't Hurting Marriage: Census figures show that fewer Americans have married since the recession begin. Many researches draws a link between falling Marriage rates and uncertain economic times. But economist Justin Wolfers argues that Marriage and divorce rates are actually immune to the vagaries of the business cycle . I'm Jennifer Ludden, and this is Talk of the Nation. But economy and troubled Marriage go together like a horse and carriage? That's what keeping hearing since the recession began. Research shows Marriage rates are down, in fact, to their lowest level in a century. Intuitively, it makes sense. Who could afford a big ceremony, far one thing? And committing to Marriage is probably easier with Job and secure future.

# CHAPTER FIVE

# TRUE COVID 19 IN 2020
# WHO IS CORONA?  WHAT IS CORONA?

**B**ut in an op-ed in the New York Times, economist Justin Wolfers warns the link does not hold up. Marriage and divorce rates. He says have been remarkably immune to the ups and downs of the business cycle. W:800-989-8255. The email address is talk @ NPR. Org. And you can join the conversation and find the link to Justin Wolfers ' op-ed,'' How Marriage survives '' at our website. Go to NPR. Org and click on Talk of the Nation. Justin Wolfers is a visiting fellow at the Brookings Institution in Washington joins us here in studio 3A. welcome. Ludden: so you write that there we re 2.1 million Marriage in- Marriage licenses-was that right-in the U.S. in 2009,and that is down a bit. You don 't think any of it's from the bad economy?

Printed in the United States
by Baker & Taylor Publisher Services